A CALM MIND

Short and Simple Everyday Self-Care Meditation for Busy People

by Cris Gabriel

A Calm Mind
Cristina Gabriel

Disclaimer
This book contains the ideas and opinions of its author. The intention of this book is to provide information, helpful content, and motivation to readers about the subjects addressed. It is published and sold with the understanding that the author is not engaged to render any type of psychological, medical, legal, or any other kind of personal or professional advice. No warranties or guarantees are expressed or implied by the author's choice to include any of the content in this volume. The author shall not be liable for any physical, psychological, emotional, financial, or commercial damages, including, but not limited to, special, incidental, consequential, or other damages. The reader is responsible for their own choices, actions, and results.

1st Edition. 1st printing 2022

Cover Concept Design and Interior Design: Charles Raywood, Oxygen Publishing Inc.
Editor: Charles Raywood

Independently Published by
Oxygen Publishing Inc.
Montreal, QC, Canada
www.oxygenpublishing.com

ISBN: 978-1-990093-37-1
Imprint: Independently published

"Calmness of mind is one of the beautiful jewels of wisdom.
It is the result of long and patient effort in self-control."

~James Allen~

Every time we practice meditation, we are generating
greater amounts of good and positive energies.

Our mind becomes calm, and we think more clearly.

The body follows and becomes calm and productive.

When our mind is calm and relaxed, we think
more positively and creatively.

When our body is calm we can move easily,
and become more energetic and productive.

Namaste
Cris Gabriel

I've experienced the magic of Cris' meditations and am so grateful to have them outlined here in this guide. She is always willing and happy to serve and now she's graciously given us her wisdom and beautiful practices wrapped up on the pages within this book.

An essential manual for anyone looking to add peace and harmony in their lives. This book is simple but powerful and if you put it into practice daily, you will discover the magic you already possess within you. You will begin living a fuller, more peaceful and complete life.

Joe Trimboli (joetrimboli.com)

It is such a joy to see this beautiful book in print! As one of Cris' students I hear her voice in every line - encouraging, supportive and compassionate. She guides us to incorporate the techniques she describes into a daily practice. Do this, and you will transform your life.

Susan Davidson

The world we inhabit is complex, and our minds often mirror its relentless pace. The twelve disarmingly simple practices outlined by Cris Gabriel provide a valuable resource to finding the stillness and calm we crave. I strongly recommend this book for everyone who has trouble finding the time to nurture themselves in mind, body and spirit.

Diane Delli Colli

TABLE OF CONTENTS

ABOUT THIS BOOK

This book is a simple and concise guide offering different ways to meditate in order to achieve a calm and productive existence. I love Bob Proctor's quote to "calm down, speed up" and this is not a contradiction. I agree with him because after my meditation practice in the morning, I start my day with a calm mind. My mind is not busy, so I can think clearly and become more creative. My mind is at one with my inner being, rather than the outside world. I can focus on the things I need to achieve with creativeness and purpose. Moreover, when our mind is calm our body follows and exudes greater energy. I calm down and I speed up, and I use as an affirmation "I am calm, and I am productive".

Everyday take a few minutes to open this book and practice your meditation. You can start or end your day with any of the mediations I have featured. You can also practice a couple minutes of meditation during your coffee, lunch or afternoon break. Sit still and bring awareness to your breath. Breathe in and out from your Hara (belly) and recite an affirmation such as "I breathe in gratitude, I breathe out gratitude." Or say any affirmations that you want to feel. In this book you will learn very simple and short meditations that will help you feel calm and relaxed even during your busiest days. Make a habit of choosing one of the twelve meditations every day. Open your mind and your heart within a serene space, and the right practice will be chosen for you. Set a pure intent, and you will receive exactly what you need in that moment of serenity.

All meditations in this book are inspired by my Yoga and Reiki practices, and learned from different meditation communities I belong to. It is a handy and concise guide to help you feel calm, relaxed and productive all at the same time.

Everyday life is so hectic and busy for most of us; dealing with work, business, family, children, household, and media, the list is never ending. If you sit and think how your day went and all the things you accomplished, you will discover how many things you were unable to complete; work at the office or at home usually dominates our day. Yet in your mind and heart you know you wanted to add some self-care, but you had little opportunity to fit it in.

There are lot's ways to practice self-care. In this book the practice I will share with you is through meditation. Calm your mind and body and feel one with your true nature. As you read and practice from this book, you are on the way to adding self-care to your list of daily priorities.

This book is for everyone, with or without previous meditation experience. The meditation practices are all short and simple to follow, and can be fitted easily into your full and productive day. Start by practicing for two or three minutes, and then add more minutes when you wish to. Because I specifically created this book for busy "productive" people like you, these short practices are easy to include within your day. They will motivate and inspire you to develop and maintain your daily self-care routine. The more you practice, the calmer and more relaxed you will become.

You can spread out your short meditation practices throughout your day whenever you want. You can make a habit of meditating for a few minutes as soon as you wake up and before you go to sleep. I truly believe that regardless of time and duration of meditation, you will get great benefits from your practice. The moment you decide to meditate, your body, mind and spirit are already open to receive. You think about the idea of meditation because you want to feel calm and relaxed. Thoughts are energy. You see the meditation in your mind's eye. Your body responds to that energy and you pick up this book and follow the steps herein. You align thoughts, feelings and actions. You show up in your practice and you confer love and care to yourself. You will feel so grateful for the results you receive from supporting your self-care. Your practice will allow you to experience the beautiful serenity space within you. You will feel calmness, peace, gratitude, abundance, joy, love and compassion.

Read the first step of each meditation. "Sit in a comfortable position in a quiet room. Place your hands together to center your mind and set an intention for your practice." The moment you set that intent, your mind, body and spirit will be in harmony with the universe. You will feel at one with the universe, and the universe will be at one with you. I truly believe that you and I together become the universe, and the universe is all of us. Set a pure intent (objective) that you will receive exactly what you need at that moment in time, and you will acquire it. You request, you believe, and you will receive. When you learn these simple and concise meditations, they will become an integral part of your self-care tool belt, that you can use them anytime and anywhere. Start your meditation journey with an open mind and an open heart. You will feel the love, joy and peace to sustain you throughout the day.

Congratulations for opening this book and making the marvelous decision to assimilate this practice in your daily life. Make it a habit of consulting it everyday, and allow yourself a few minutes to sit and compose yourself in a comfortable position. Select a meditation that resonates with you at that moment. When you are ready, start your practice and dedicate a few minutes to sit in stillness and concentration.

This book should become your everyday companion. Give yourself the gift of a few minutes of stillness and concentration every day, and you will be happy that you did. You will develop a calm mind every time you practice. A calm mind promotes a calm body and a calm spirit. My pure intent of writing this book is to help you bring calmness in your busy day, and create a habit of practicing meditation as part of your daily routine. The beauty of these twelve daily meditations is their simplicity, short duration and intuitive nature. One of my favorites is the walking meditation. When I walk my dog in the woods I let him enjoy being at one with nature. I feel the same, that I too am at one with nature, and simultaneously at one with my breathing while we walk. The next time you go out for a walk bring awareness to your breathing as you step along the path. The nature around you brings calmness to your mind, and coupled with your breathing awareness, will complete your meditation practice. Even a short walk will give you benefits. All the meditations featured in my book provide suggestions on how you can incorporate them in your daily activities.

MEDITATION #1: HARA

"Hara is the home of our true nature.
Our true nature has no anger, no
worries and fear. It's pure love,
compassion, faith and gratitude."

Hara

Hara simply means belly as translated from Japanese.

5 short and simple steps:

1. Sit in a comfortable position in a quiet room. Place your hands together to center your mind and set an intention for your practice.

2. Place your hands on your lap. Feel your breath, and with the next inhale lengthen your spine, and when you exhale relax your shoulders. Stay in this position throughout your practice whilst easy breathing.

3. Now bring awareness to your Hara. It's located just below your belly button. Breathe in through your nose, and feel the energy moving down to the Hara as your belly rises. Breathe out through your nose as the belly falls, and feel the expansion of breath throughout your body.

4. Continue for a few minutes and add extra minutes, as you feel guided.

5. End the practice with gratitude, with hands together saying "thank you".

Incorporate this meditation into your daily activities

- Upon waking up and before getting out of the bed, place both hands on your Hara. Breathe in and out in your Hara three times, and feel that beautiful energy you have within.

- During a coffee or tea break take a moment to bring your awareness to your Hara, just below your belly button. Breathe in and out three times, and you will feel the calmness within. Enjoy your coffee or tea!

- Before you sleep breathe in and out in your Hara three times and visualize all the blessings and abundance you received today. Fall asleep with a calm mind and you will have a peaceful night.

On the following pages journal your daily experience practicing the Hara meditation for the next 30 days

Day 1

_____

_____

_____

_____

_____

_____

_____

_____

_____

_____

Day 2

_____

_____

_____

_____

_____

_____

_____

_____

_____

_____

Day 3

_____

_____

_____

_____

_____

_____

_____

_____

_____

_____

Day 4

_____

_____

_____

_____

_____

_____

_____

_____

_____

_____

_____

Day 5

_____
_____
_____
_____
_____
_____
_____
_____
_____

Day 6

_____
_____
_____
_____
_____
_____
_____
_____
_____
_____
_____

Day 7 _____

_____

_____

_____

_____

_____

_____

_____

_____

Day 8 _____

_____

_____

_____

_____

_____

_____

_____

_____

Day 9 _____

_____

_____

_____

_____

_____

_____

_____

_____

Day 10 _____

_____

_____

_____

_____

_____

_____

_____

_____

_____

Day 11 _____

_____

_____

_____

_____

_____

_____

_____

_____

_____

_____

_____

Day 12 _____

_____

_____

_____

_____

_____

_____

_____

_____

_____

_____

_____

Day 13 _____

_____

_____

_____

_____

_____

_____

_____

_____

Day 14 _____

_____

_____

_____

_____

_____

_____

_____

_____

Day 15

_____

_____

_____

_____

_____

_____

_____

_____

_____

_____

_____

Day 16

_____

_____

_____

_____

_____

_____

_____

_____

_____

_____

_____

Day 17 _____

_____

_____

_____

_____

_____

_____

_____

_____

_____

Day 18 _____

_____

_____

_____

_____

_____

_____

_____

_____

_____

Day 19

Day 20

Day 21

Day 22

Day 23 _____

_____

_____

_____

_____

_____

_____

_____

_____

_____

_____

Day 24 _____

_____

_____

_____

_____

_____

_____

_____

_____

_____

_____

Day 25 _____

_____
_____
_____
_____
_____
_____
_____
_____

Day 26 _____

_____
_____
_____
_____
_____
_____
_____
_____

Day 27

_____

_____

_____

_____

_____

_____

_____

_____

_____

_____

Day 28

_____

_____

_____

_____

_____

_____

_____

_____

_____

_____

Day 29

_____

_____

_____

_____

_____

_____

_____

_____

_____

Day 30

_____

_____

_____

_____

_____

_____

_____

_____

_____

MEDITATION #2:
HARA & VISUALIZATION

"The more light you allow within you, the
brighter the world you live in will be"

~Shakti~

Hara and Visualization

Visualization is the formation of mental images.

5 short and simple steps:

1. Sit in a comfortable position in a quiet room. Place your hands together to center your mind and set an intention for your practice.

2. Place your hands on your lap. Feel your breath, and with the next inhale lengthen your spine, and when you exhale relax your shoulders. Stay in this position throughout your practice whilst easy breathing.

3. Breathe into your Hara and visualize a glowing luminous bright sphere within your Hara. Breathe out and the glowing luminous bright sphere expands throughout your body.

4. Continue for a few minutes and add extra minutes, as you feel guided.

5. End the practice with gratitude, with hands together saying "thank you".

Incorporate this meditation into your daily activities

- Upon waking up and before getting out of the bed, place both hands on your Hara. Breathe in and out in your Hara three times. Visualize a glowing sphere within your Hara expanding and flowing through you.

- During mini breaks sit and relax, breathe in and out in your Hara three times and visualize the glowing sphere in your Hara. In just three rounds of breath, you will feel grounded and calm.

- Before you sleep breath in and out in your Hara three times and visualize a glowing sphere in your Hara expanding and flowing through you. Imagine your whole body is filled with bright light, and you will feel calm and fall asleep relaxed.

On the following pages journal your daily experience practicing the Hara & Visualization meditation for the next 30 days

Day 1

_____

_____

_____

_____

_____

_____

_____

_____

_____

_____

Day 2

_____

_____

_____

_____

_____

_____

_____

_____

_____

_____

_____

Day 3

_____

_____

_____

_____

_____

_____

_____

_____

_____

Day 4

_____

_____

_____

_____

_____

_____

_____

_____

_____

_____

_____

_____

_____

Day 5

_____

_____

_____

_____

_____

_____

_____

_____

_____

_____

Day 6

_____

_____

_____

_____

_____

_____

_____

_____

_____

_____

_____

Day 7

_____

_____

_____

_____

_____

_____

_____

_____

_____

Day 8

_____

_____

_____

_____

_____

_____

_____

_____

_____

_____

_____

_____

Day 9

_____

_____

_____

_____

_____

_____

_____

_____

_____

_____

Day 10

_____

_____

_____

_____

_____

_____

_____

_____

_____

_____

_____

_____

Day 11

_____

_____

_____

_____

_____

_____

_____

_____

_____

_____

Day 12

_____

_____

_____

_____

_____

_____

_____

_____

_____

_____

_____

_____

Day 13

_____

_____

_____

_____

_____

_____

_____

_____

_____

_____

Day 14

_____

_____

_____

_____

_____

_____

_____

_____

_____

_____

Day 15

_____

_____

_____

_____

_____

_____

_____

_____

_____

Day 16

_____

_____

_____

_____

_____

_____

_____

_____

_____

_____

_____

Day 17

_____

_____

_____

_____

_____

_____

_____

_____

_____

_____

_____

Day 18

_____

_____

_____

_____

_____

_____

_____

_____

_____

_____

_____

_____

Day 19 _____

_____

_____

_____

_____

_____

_____

_____

_____

Day 20 _____

_____

_____

_____

_____

_____

_____

_____

_____

Day 21

_____
_____
_____
_____
_____
_____
_____
_____
_____

Day 22

_____
_____
_____
_____
_____
_____
_____
_____
_____
_____
_____
_____

Day 23

_____

_____

_____

_____

_____

_____

_____

_____

Day 24

_____

_____

_____

_____

_____

_____

_____

_____

_____

_____

Day 25 _____

_____

_____

_____

_____

_____

_____

_____

_____

_____

_____

Day 26 _____

_____

_____

_____

_____

_____

_____

_____

_____

_____

_____

Day 27

Day 28

Day 29

Day 30

MEDITATION #3: VISUALIZATION

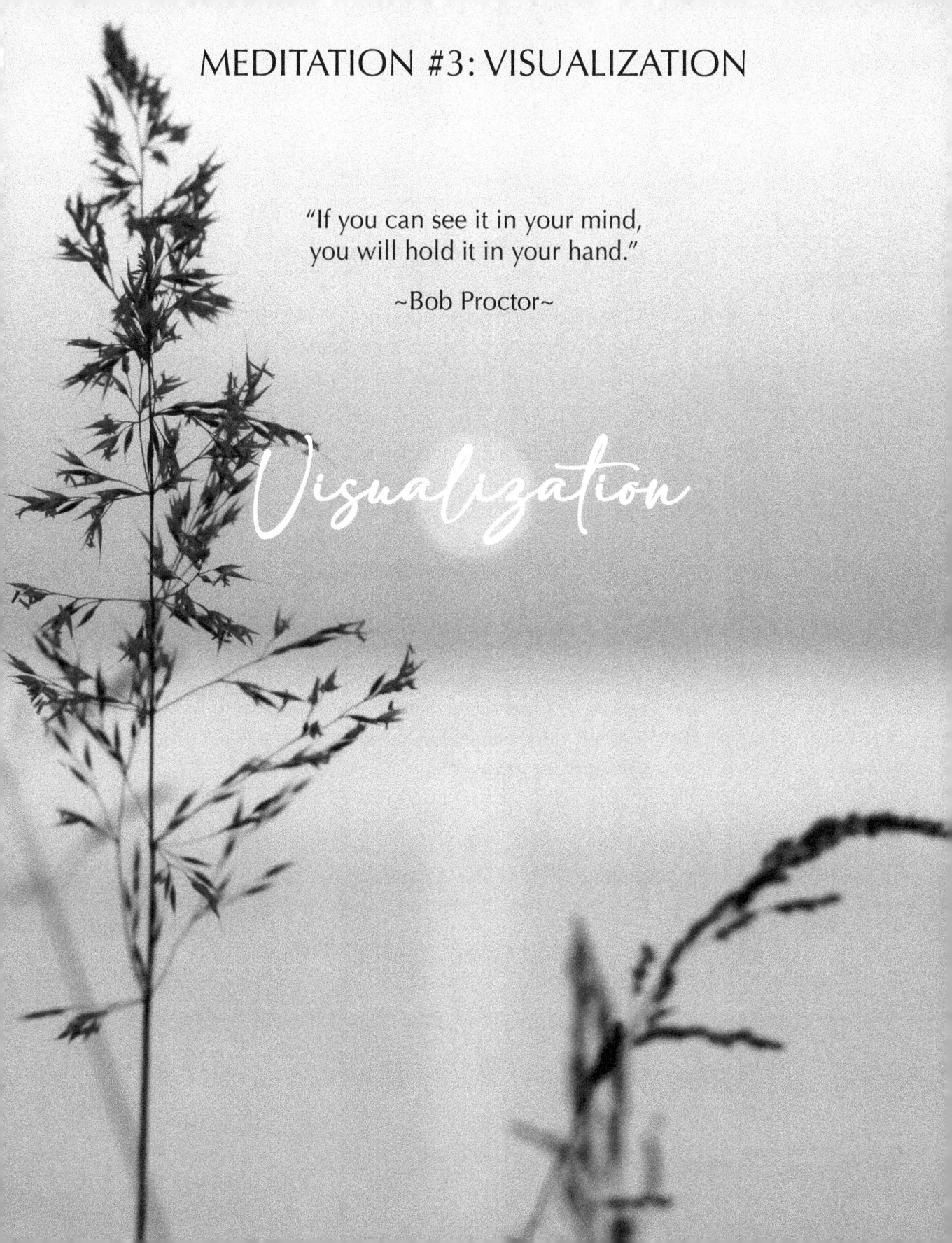

"If you can see it in your mind,
you will hold it in your hand."

~Bob Proctor~

Visualization

Visualization is the formation of mental images.

5 short and simple steps:

1. Sit in a comfortable position in a quiet room. Place your hands together to center your mind and set an intention for your practice.

2. Place your hands on your lap. Feel your breath, and with the next inhale lengthen your spine, and when you exhale relax your shoulders. Stay in this position throughout your practice whilst easy breathing.

3. Breathe in and out in your Hara, and start to visualize something that you love to do; that makes you feel relaxed and happy. Perhaps, looking at the ocean, listening to the sounds of nature, or having a spa.

4. Continue for a few minutes and add extra minutes, as you feel guided.

5. End the practice with gratitude, with hands together saying "thank you".

Incorporate this meditation into your daily activities

- Upon waking up and before getting out of the bed, place both hands on your Hara. Breathe in and out in your Hara three times. Visualize yourself having a calm and productive day, or anything you want to declare.

- During mini breaks sit and relax, breathe in and out in your Hara three times, and visualize things that make you happy, calm and relaxed.

- Before you sleep breathe in and out in your Hara three times and visualize all the blessings and abundance you received today.

On the following pages journal your daily experience practicing the Visualization meditation for the next 30 days

Day 1 _____

_____

_____

_____

_____

_____

_____

_____

_____

_____

_____

Day 2 _____

_____

_____

_____

_____

_____

_____

_____

_____

_____

_____

Day 3

_____

_____

_____

_____

_____

_____

_____

_____

_____

_____

Day 4

_____

_____

_____

_____

_____

_____

_____

_____

_____

_____

Day 5

_____
_____
_____
_____
_____
_____
_____
_____
_____
_____

Day 6

_____
_____
_____
_____
_____
_____
_____
_____
_____
_____

Day 7

_____

_____

_____

_____

_____

_____

_____

_____

_____

_____

Day 8

_____

_____

_____

_____

_____

_____

_____

_____

_____

_____

Day 9

_____
_____
_____
_____
_____
_____
_____
_____
_____
_____

Day 10

_____
_____
_____
_____
_____
_____
_____
_____
_____
_____

Day 11

_____

_____

_____

_____

_____

_____

_____

_____

_____

_____

_____

Day 12

_____

_____

_____

_____

_____

_____

_____

_____

_____

_____

_____

Day 13

_____
_____
_____
_____
_____
_____
_____
_____
_____
_____

Day 14

_____
_____
_____
_____
_____
_____
_____
_____
_____

Day 15 _____

_____

_____

_____

_____

_____

_____

_____

_____

Day 16 _____

_____

_____

_____

_____

_____

_____

_____

_____

Day 17

_____

_____

_____

_____

_____

_____

_____

_____

_____

_____

Day 18

_____

_____

_____

_____

_____

_____

_____

_____

_____

_____

Day 19 _____

_____

_____

_____

_____

_____

_____

_____

_____

Day 20 _____

_____

_____

_____

_____

_____

_____

_____

_____

Day 21

Day 22

Day 23 _____

_____

_____

_____

_____

_____

_____

_____

_____

_____

Day 24 _____

_____

_____

_____

_____

_____

_____

_____

_____

_____

Day 25 _____

_____

_____

_____

_____

_____

_____

_____

_____

_____

_____

Day 26 _____

_____

_____

_____

_____

_____

_____

_____

_____

_____

_____

Day 27

_____

_____

_____

_____

_____

_____

_____

_____

Day 28

_____

_____

_____

_____

_____

_____

_____

_____

_____

Day 29

_____

Day 30

_____

MEDITATION #4: ZAZEN

"In Zazen, leave your front door and your
back door open. Let thoughts come
and go. Just don't serve them tea."

~Shunryu Suzuki~

Zazen

Zazen means simple sitting meditation and allows the mind to flow with thoughts without judgment and involvement.

5 short and simple steps:

1. Sit in a comfortable position in a quiet room. Place your hands together to center your mind and set an intention for your practice.

2. Place your hands on your lap. Feel your breath, and with the next inhale lengthen your spine, and when you exhale relax your shoulders. Stay in this position throughout your practice whilst easy breathing.

3. Breathe in and out in your Hara. Imagine your mind has an open front door and an open back door. Every thought that comes through the front door let it out through the back door, without entertaining it or becoming involved. Continue the practice without judgment and your mind will start to soften.

4. Continue for a few minutes and add extra minutes, as you feel guided.

5. End the practice with gratitude, with hands together saying "thank you".

Incorporate this meditation into your daily activities

- Upon waking up before getting out of the bed, take a slow and deep breath in and breathe out through your nose. Let your thoughts come and go.

- During mini breaks sit and relax, and take a slow and deep breath in and breathe out through your nose. Let your thoughts come and go.

- Before you sleep take a slow and deep breath in and breathe out through your nose three times. Let your thoughts come and go. Declare your gratitude for the day.

On the following pages journal your daily experience practicing the Zazen meditation for the next 30 days

Day 1

_____

_____

_____

_____

_____

_____

_____

_____

_____

_____

_____

_____

_____

Day 2

_____

_____

_____

_____

_____

_____

_____

_____

_____

_____

_____

_____

_____

Day 3

_____

_____

_____

_____

_____

_____

_____

_____

_____

Day 4

_____

_____

_____

_____

_____

_____

_____

_____

_____

_____

Day 5

_____

_____

_____

_____

_____

_____

_____

_____

_____

_____

Day 6

_____

_____

_____

_____

_____

_____

_____

_____

_____

Day 7 _____

_____

_____

_____

_____

_____

_____

_____

_____

_____

Day 8 _____

_____

_____

_____

_____

_____

_____

_____

_____

_____

Day 9

_____

_____

_____

_____

_____

_____

_____

_____

_____

_____

_____

Day 10

_____

_____

_____

_____

_____

_____

_____

_____

_____

_____

_____

Day 11 _____

_____

_____

_____

_____

_____

_____

_____

_____

_____

_____

Day 12 _____

_____

_____

_____

_____

_____

_____

_____

_____

_____

Day 13

_____
_____
_____
_____
_____
_____
_____
_____
_____
_____
_____
_____
_____
_____

Day 14

_____
_____
_____
_____
_____
_____
_____
_____
_____
_____
_____
_____
_____

Day 15

_____

Day 16

_____

Day 17

_____

_____

_____

_____

_____

_____

_____

_____

_____

_____

Day 18

_____

_____

_____

_____

_____

_____

_____

_____

_____

_____

_____

Day 19

_____

_____

_____

_____

_____

_____

_____

_____

Day 20

_____

_____

_____

_____

_____

_____

_____

_____

_____

Day 21

_____

Day 22

_____

Day 23 _____

_____

_____

_____

_____

_____

_____

_____

_____

_____

Day 24 _____

_____

_____

_____

_____

_____

_____

_____

_____

_____

_____

Day 25 _____

_____

_____

_____

_____

_____

_____

_____

_____

_____

Day 26 _____

_____

_____

_____

_____

_____

_____

_____

_____

_____

_____

Day 27 _____

_____
_____
_____
_____
_____
_____
_____
_____
_____

Day 28 _____

_____
_____
_____
_____
_____
_____
_____
_____
_____
_____
_____

Day 29 _____

_____

_____

_____

_____

_____

_____

_____

_____

_____

Day 30 _____

_____

_____

_____

_____

_____

_____

_____

_____

_____

MEDITATION #5: BODY SCAN

"Listen to your body and listen to the
messages from your body.
You will feel one with yourself
during body scan."

Body Scan

MEDITATION #5: BODY SCAN

Body scan is bringing awareness to your body and noticing the sensation.

5 short and simple steps:

1. Sit in a comfortable position in a quiet room. Place your hands together to center your mind and set an intention for your practice.

2. Place your hands on your lap. Feel your breath, and with the next inhale lengthen your spine, and when you exhale relax your shoulders. Stay in this position throughout your practice whilst easy breathing.

3. Breathe in and out in your Hara and start scanning your body. You may start from your feet all the way up to your head, or you can start from your head all the way down to your feet. During the body scan notice and feel the sensation of each part of your body. Don't judge or analyze, just be aware of your breathing and the sensations you discover.

4. Continue for a few minutes and add extra minutes, as you feel guided.

5. End the practice with gratitude, with hands together saying "thank you".

Incorporate this meditation into your daily activities

- Upon waking up before getting out of the bed, take a slow and deep breath in and out through your nose three times. Make a quick body scan from your feet to your head. Say "thank you" to your body.

- During mini breaks sit and relax. Take a slow and deep breath in and out through your nose three times. Make a quick scan of your body.

- Before you go to sleep take a slow and deep breath in and out through your nose three times. In bed relax your body and start to scan from your feet to head or head to feet. You might fall asleep in the middle of your scanning and that is a wonderful gift!

On the following pages journal your daily experience practicing the Body Scan meditation for the next 30 days

Day 1

_____

_____

_____

_____

_____

_____

_____

_____

_____

_____

_____

_____

Day 2

_____

_____

_____

_____

_____

_____

_____

_____

_____

_____

_____

_____

_____

Day 3

Day 4

Day 5

_____

_____

_____

_____

_____

_____

_____

_____

_____

_____

Day 6

_____

_____

_____

_____

_____

_____

_____

_____

_____

_____

_____

Day 7

_____

Day 8

_____

Day 9 _____

_____

_____

_____

_____

_____

_____

_____

_____

Day 10 _____

_____

_____

_____

_____

_____

_____

_____

_____

_____

Day 11

_____

_____

_____

_____

_____

_____

_____

_____

_____

_____

Day 12

_____

_____

_____

_____

_____

_____

_____

_____

_____

_____

Day 13 _____

_____

_____

_____

_____

_____

_____

_____

_____

_____

Day 14 _____

_____

_____

_____

_____

_____

_____

_____

_____

_____

_____

Day 15

_____

Day 16

_____

Day 17

_____

_____

_____

_____

_____

_____

_____

_____

_____

_____

_____

Day 18

_____

_____

_____

_____

_____

_____

_____

_____

_____

_____

_____

Day 19 _____

_____

_____

_____

_____

_____

_____

_____

_____

_____

_____

Day 20 _____

_____

_____

_____

_____

_____

_____

_____

_____

_____

_____

_____

Day 21

_____

_____

_____

_____

_____

_____

_____

_____

_____

Day 22

_____

_____

_____

_____

_____

_____

_____

_____

_____

_____

Day 23 _____

_____

_____

_____

_____

_____

_____

_____

_____

_____

Day 24 _____

_____

_____

_____

_____

_____

_____

_____

_____

_____

Day 25

_____
_____
_____
_____
_____
_____
_____
_____
_____

Day 26

_____
_____
_____
_____
_____
_____
_____
_____
_____
_____

Day 27

_____

Day 28

_____

Day 29

_____

_____

_____

_____

_____

_____

_____

_____

_____

_____

Day 30

_____

_____

_____

_____

_____

_____

_____

_____

_____

_____

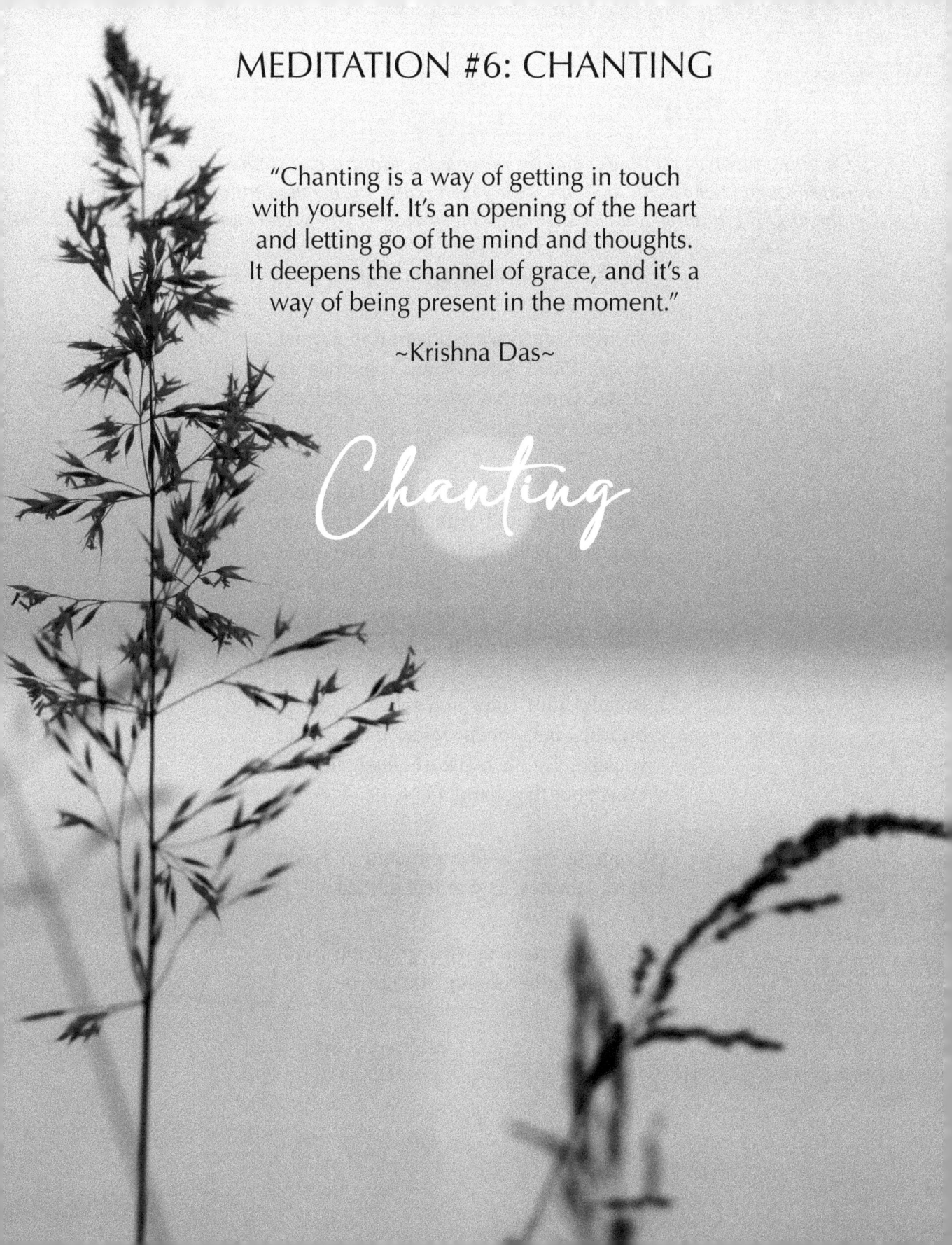

MEDITATION #6: CHANTING

"Chanting is a way of getting in touch
with yourself. It's an opening of the heart
and letting go of the mind and thoughts.
It deepens the channel of grace, and it's a
way of being present in the moment."

~Krishna Das~

Chanting

MEDITATION #6: CHANTING

Chanting involves reciting a mantra repeatedly. Mantra is a sound that vocalizes out through your mouth together with your breath. In this meditation we will use the O U E I mantra. You can also use other mantras you prefer in this practice.

5 short and simple steps:

1. Sit in a comfortable position in a quiet room. Place your hands together to center your mind and set an intention for your practice.

2. Place your hands on your lap. Feel your breath, and with the next inhale lengthen your spine, and when you exhale relax your shoulders. Stay in this position throughout your practice whilst easy breathing.

3. Breathe into Hara and when ready to breathe out, open your mouth and vocalize O U E I. Breathe in again and breath out the chant O U E I.

4. Continue for a few minutes and add extra minutes, as you feel guided.

5. End the practice with gratitude, with hands together saying "thank you".

Incorporate this meditation into your daily activities

- Upon waking up before getting out of the bed, take a slow and deep breath in and out through your nose. In your mind's eye recite or chant the O U E I mantra. Repeat the mantra three to six rounds. You can use the O U E I mantra or choose another that you like. Be at one with your Hara as you chant.

- During mini breaks sit and relax. Take a slow and deep breath in and out through your nose. In your mind's eye recite or chant the mantra between three to six rounds. Use a mantra that resonates with you in that moment in time.

- Before you go to sleep, take a slow and deep breath in and out through your nose three times. Chant the mantra through your minds eyes for a few rounds. As you chant you will calm your mind and help you to sleep peacefully.

On the following pages journal your daily experience practicing the Chanting meditation for the next 30 days

Day 1 _____

_____

_____

_____

_____

_____

_____

_____

_____

_____

_____

Day 2 _____

_____

_____

_____

_____

_____

_____

_____

_____

_____

_____

_____

Day 3

_____

_____

_____

_____

_____

_____

_____

_____

_____

Day 4

_____

_____

_____

_____

_____

_____

_____

_____

_____

_____

_____

Day 5

_____
_____
_____
_____
_____
_____
_____
_____
_____
_____

Day 6

_____
_____
_____
_____
_____
_____
_____
_____
_____
_____
_____
_____

Day 7

_____

_____

_____

_____

_____

_____

_____

_____

_____

Day 8

_____

_____

_____

_____

_____

_____

_____

_____

_____

_____

Day 9

_____

_____

_____

_____

_____

_____

_____

_____

_____

_____

Day 10

_____

_____

_____

_____

_____

_____

_____

_____

_____

_____

_____

Day 11

_____

_____

_____

_____

_____

_____

_____

_____

_____

Day 12

_____

_____

_____

_____

_____

_____

_____

_____

_____

_____

_____

_____

Day 13

_____

_____

_____

_____

_____

_____

_____

_____

_____

Day 14

_____

_____

_____

_____

_____

_____

_____

_____

_____

_____

Day 15 _____

_____

_____

_____

_____

_____

_____

_____

_____

_____

Day 16 _____

_____

_____

_____

_____

_____

_____

_____

_____

_____

_____

Day 17

Day 18

Day 19 _____

_____

_____

_____

_____

_____

_____

_____

_____

_____

Day 20 _____

_____

_____

_____

_____

_____

_____

_____

_____

_____

_____

_____

Day 21

_____

_____

_____

_____

_____

_____

_____

_____

_____

_____

Day 22

_____

_____

_____

_____

_____

_____

_____

_____

_____

_____

Day 23

_____

Day 24

_____

Day 25

_____

_____

_____

_____

_____

_____

_____

_____

_____

_____

Day 26

_____

_____

_____

_____

_____

_____

_____

_____

_____

_____

_____

Day 27 _____

_____

_____

_____

_____

_____

_____

_____

_____

_____

Day 28 _____

_____

_____

_____

_____

_____

_____

_____

_____

_____

_____

Day 29
_____

_____
_____
_____
_____
_____
_____
_____
_____

Day 30
_____
_____
_____
_____
_____
_____
_____
_____
_____
_____

MEDITATION #7: HARA FLOW

"Flow the energy coming from the Hara
throughout your body and feel
the spiritual blessing flowing
into and through you."

Hara Flow

Hara flow is a combination of belly breathing and gentle movement.

5 short and simple steps:

1. Sit in a comfortable position in a quiet room. Place your hands together to center your mind and set an intention for your practice.

2. Place your hands on your lap. Feel your breath, and with the next inhale lengthen your spine, and when you exhale relax your shoulders. Stay in this position throughout your practice whilst easy breathing.

3. Breathe into Hara and move your arms up. Breathe out to your Hara and bring your arms down. With your next breath in move any part of your body gently, and when breathing out return your body to its original position. Listen to your body and your body will tell you which part it needs to move next.

4. Continue for a few minutes and add extra minutes, as you feel guided.

5. End the practice with gratitude, with hands together saying "thank you".

Incorporate this meditation into your daily activities

- Upon waking up before getting out of the bed, take a slow and deep breath in your Hara and flow your arms up. Exhale through your Hara and flow your arms down. Repeat three times.

- During mini breaks sit or stand and relax. Take a slow and deep breath in and flow your arms up. Exhale through your Hara and flow your arms down. Repeat three times.

- Before you go to bed stand or sit and relax your body. Take a slow and deep breath in your Hara and flow your arms up. Exhale through your Hara and flow your arms down. Repeat three times.

On the following pages journal your daily experience practicing the Hara Flow meditation for the next 30 days

Day 1

_____
_____
_____
_____
_____
_____
_____
_____
_____
_____

Day 2

_____
_____
_____
_____
_____
_____
_____
_____
_____

Day 3 _____

_____

_____

_____

_____

_____

_____

_____

_____

_____

_____

Day 4 _____

_____

_____

_____

_____

_____

_____

_____

_____

_____

_____

Day 5 _____

_____

_____

_____

_____

_____

_____

_____

_____

_____

Day 6 _____

_____

_____

_____

_____

_____

_____

_____

_____

_____

Day 7

_____

Day 8

_____

Day 9

_____

_____

_____

_____

_____

_____

_____

_____

_____

Day 10

_____

_____

_____

_____

_____

_____

_____

_____

_____

Day 11

Day 12

Day 13

_____

_____

_____

_____

_____

_____

_____

_____

Day 14

_____

_____

_____

_____

_____

_____

_____

_____

Day 15

Day 16

Day 17 _____

_____

_____

_____

_____

_____

_____

_____

_____

_____

Day 18 _____

_____

_____

_____

_____

_____

_____

_____

_____

_____

Day 19

_____

Day 20

_____

Day 21 _____

_____

_____

_____

_____

_____

_____

_____

_____

_____

_____

Day 22 _____

_____

_____

_____

_____

_____

_____

_____

_____

_____

_____

Day 23 _____

_____

_____

_____

_____

_____

_____

_____

_____

_____

Day 24 _____

_____

_____

_____

_____

_____

_____

_____

_____

Day 25

_____

_____

_____

_____

_____

_____

_____

_____

Day 26

_____

_____

_____

_____

_____

_____

_____

_____

Day 27

Day 28

Day 29

_____

_____

_____

_____

_____

_____

_____

_____

_____

Day 30

_____

_____

_____

_____

_____

_____

_____

_____

_____

"Loving and compassionate touch is a
like a warm hug. It's calming and pure."

Hands-on Healing

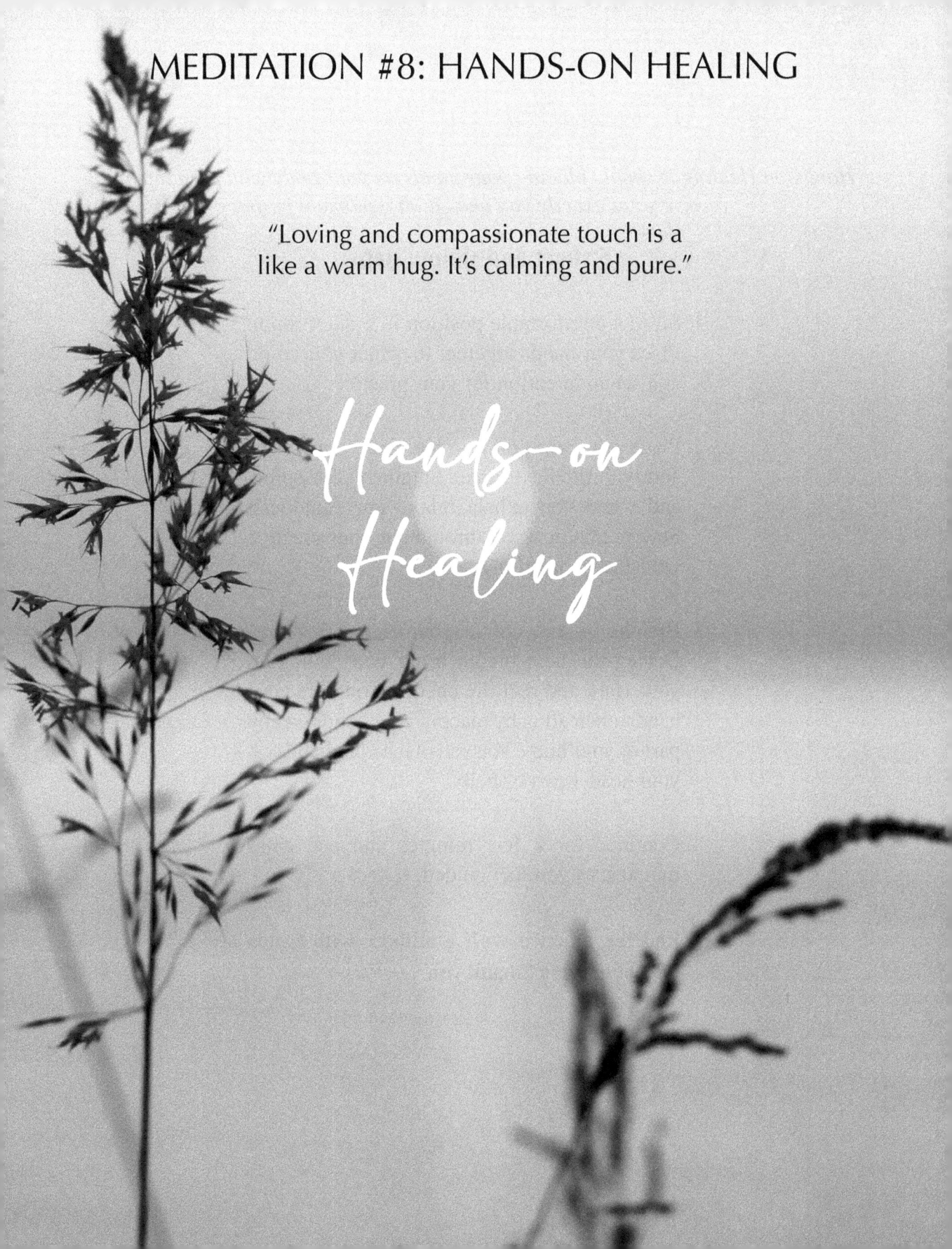

MEDITATION #8: HANDS-ON HEALING

Hands-on Healing is simply placing your hands on your body with pure intent to receive what exactly you need at that moment in time.

5 short and simple steps:

1. Sit in a comfortable position in a quiet room. Place your hands together to center your mind and set an intention for your practice.

2. Place your hands on your lap. Feel your breath, and with the next inhale lengthen your spine, and when you exhale relax your shoulders. Stay in this position throughout your practice whilst easy breathing.

3. Breathe in and out in your Hara six times. During the next breath bring your hands on your Hara and feel the energy. Continue your hands-on healing by placing your hands on any part of your body. You can place your hands on your head, heart or belly.

4. Continue for a few minutes and add extra minutes, as you feel guided.

5. End the practice with gratitude, with hands together saying "thank you".

Incorporate this meditation into your daily activities

- Upon waking up rest in your bed for two minutes. Place one hand on your Hara and one hand on your heart. Take a slow deep breath in through your nose, and out through your nose. Feel one with your Hara.

- During mini breaks sit and relax. Place your hand on your heart or belly and breath in and out through the nose. You can also do a hand's off healing by just sitting and relaxing and feeling the energy coming from your hands.

- Before you go to sleep lie down on your bed. Place your hand on your heart and belly or any other part of the body that you feel needs a healing touch. Bring awareness to your breath and feel one with your Hara. You may fall asleep while doing this, and it's a wonderful experience to sleep with a beautiful energy flowing into and through you.

On the following pages journal your daily experience practicing the Hands-on Healing meditation for the next 30 days

Day 1

_____
_____
_____
_____
_____
_____
_____
_____
_____
_____
_____
_____

Day 2

_____
_____
_____
_____
_____
_____
_____
_____
_____
_____
_____
_____

Day 3

_____

_____

_____

_____

_____

_____

_____

_____

Day 4

_____

_____

_____

_____

_____

_____

_____

_____

Day 5

_____

_____

_____

_____

_____

_____

_____

_____

_____

_____

Day 6

_____

_____

_____

_____

_____

_____

_____

_____

_____

_____

_____

Day 7

Day 8

Day 9

_____

_____

_____

_____

_____

_____

_____

_____

_____

_____

Day 10

_____

_____

_____

_____

_____

_____

_____

_____

_____

_____

_____

Day 11

_____

Day 12

Day 13 _____

_____

_____

_____

_____

_____

_____

_____

_____

_____

Day 14 _____

_____

_____

_____

_____

_____

_____

_____

_____

_____

Day 15

Day 16

Day 17 _____

_____

_____

_____

_____

_____

_____

_____

_____

_____

Day 18 _____

_____

_____

_____

_____

_____

_____

_____

_____

_____

_____

Day 19

Day 20

Day 21

_____
_____
_____
_____
_____
_____
_____
_____
_____
_____

Day 22

_____
_____
_____
_____
_____
_____
_____
_____
_____
_____

Day 23

_____

_____

_____

_____

_____

_____

_____

_____

Day 24

_____

_____

_____

_____

_____

_____

_____

_____

_____

Day 25

Day 26

Day 27

_____

_____

_____

_____

_____

_____

_____

_____

_____

_____

Day 28

_____

_____

_____

_____

_____

_____

_____

_____

_____

_____

_____

Day 29

_____

Day 30

_____

MEDITATION #9: LOVE

"To surround yourself with love,
give yourself love first.
Breathe in love and breathe out love."

Love

MEDITATION #9: LOVE

Embody love through this simple meditation.
In every breath feel love for yourself and others.

5 short and simple steps:

1. Sit in a comfortable position in a quiet room. Place your hands together to center your mind and set an intention for your practice.

2. Place your hands on your lap. Feel your breath, and with the next inhale lengthen your spine, and when you exhale relax your shoulders. Stay in this position throughout your practice whilst easy breathing.

3. Breathe into your Hara and say, "I breathe in love". Breathe out to your Hara and say, "I breathe out love". Breathe in and out with the intent of pure love. Impress love to your heart and feel it in your entire body.

4. Continue for a few minutes and add extra minutes, as you feel guided.

5. End the practice with gratitude, with hands together saying "thank you".

Incorporate this meditation into your daily activities

- Upon waking up rest in your bed for two minutes. Place your hand on your heart and take a nice slow and deep breath in and say, "I breathe in love". Breathe out and say, "I breathe out love". Repeat for three to six rounds.

- During mini breaks sit and relax. Take a moment and bring awareness to your breath. As you breathe in say silently, "I breathe in love". Breathe out and say, "I breathe out love". Repeat for three to six rounds.

- Before you go to sleep lie down on your bed. Place your hand in your heart and as you breathe in say, "I breathe in love". As you breath out say, "I breathe out love". Repeat for three to six rounds

On the following pages journal your daily experience practicing the Love meditation for the next 30 days

Day 1

_____

_____

_____

_____

_____

_____

_____

_____

_____

_____

Day 2

_____

_____

_____

_____

_____

_____

_____

_____

_____

_____

Day 3

_____

Day 4

_____

Day 5

_____

_____

_____

_____

_____

_____

_____

_____

_____

_____

Day 6

_____

_____

_____

_____

_____

_____

_____

_____

_____

_____

_____

Day 7

_____

_____

_____

_____

_____

_____

_____

_____

_____

_____

Day 8

_____

_____

_____

_____

_____

_____

_____

_____

_____

_____

_____

Day 9

_____
_____
_____
_____
_____
_____
_____
_____
_____
_____

Day 10

_____
_____
_____
_____
_____
_____
_____
_____
_____
_____
_____

Day 11

Day 12

Day 13 _____

_____

_____

_____

_____

_____

_____

_____

_____

_____

Day 14 _____

_____

_____

_____

_____

_____

_____

_____

_____

_____

Day 15 _____

_____

_____

_____

_____

_____

_____

_____

_____

_____

_____

Day 16 _____

_____

_____

_____

_____

_____

_____

_____

_____

_____

_____

Day 17

_____

_____

_____

_____

_____

_____

_____

_____

_____

_____

Day 18

_____

_____

_____

_____

_____

_____

_____

_____

_____

_____

Day 19

Day 20

Day 21

_____

_____

_____

_____

_____

_____

_____

_____

_____

_____

Day 22

_____

_____

_____

_____

_____

_____

_____

_____

_____

_____

_____

Day 23

Day 24

Day 25

_____

_____

_____

_____

_____

_____

_____

_____

_____

_____

_____

Day 26

_____

_____

_____

_____

_____

_____

_____

_____

_____

_____

_____

Day 27

Day 28

Day 29

Day 30

MEDITATION #10: GRATITUDE

"Gratitude is an attitude that hooks us up to our source of supply. And the more grateful you are, the closer you become to your maker, to the architect of the universe, to the spiritual core of your being. It's a phenomenal lesson."

~Bob Proctor~

Gratitude

MEDITATION #10: GRATITUDE

Embody gratitude through this simple meditation. In every breath feel grateful for everything you have and everything to come.

5 short and simple steps:

1. Sit in a comfortable position in a quiet room. Place your hands together to center your mind and set an intention for your practice.

2. Place your hands on your lap. Feel your breath, and with the next inhale lengthen your spine, and when you exhale relax your shoulders. Stay in this position throughout your practice whilst easy breathing.

3. Breathe into your Hara and say, "I breathe in gratitude". Breathe out to your Hara and say, "I breathe out gratitude" Every breath in and out is with the intent of pure gratitude. Impress gratitude to your heart and feel it in your entire body.

4. Continue for a few minutes and add extra minutes, as you feel guided.

5. End the practice with gratitude, with hands together saying "thank you".

Incorporate this meditation into your daily activities

- Upon waking up rest in your bed for two minutes. Place your hand in your heart and take a nice slow and deep breath in and say, " I breathe in gratitude". As you breath out say, "I breathe out gratitude." Repeat for three to six rounds.

- During mini breaks sit and relax. Take a moment and bring awareness to your breath. As you breathe in silently say, "I breathe in gratitude". As you breath out say, "I breathe out gratitude". Repeat for three to six rounds.

- Before you go to sleep lie down on your bed. Place your hand in your heart and as you breathe in say," I breathe in gratitude". As you breath out say, "I breathe out gratitude". Continue for three to six rounds.

On the following pages journal your daily experience practicing the Gratitude meditation for the next 30 days

Day 1

_____

_____

_____

_____

_____

_____

_____

_____

_____

_____

Day 2

_____

_____

_____

_____

_____

_____

_____

_____

_____

_____

_____

Day 3

_____

_____

_____

_____

_____

_____

_____

_____

Day 4

_____

_____

_____

_____

_____

_____

_____

_____

_____

_____

_____

Day 5

_____
_____
_____
_____
_____
_____
_____
_____
_____
_____
_____

Day 6

_____
_____
_____
_____
_____
_____
_____
_____
_____
_____
_____
_____

Day 7

_____

_____

_____

_____

_____

_____

_____

_____

_____

_____

_____

Day 8

_____

_____

_____

_____

_____

_____

_____

_____

_____

_____

_____

_____

_____

Day 9 _____

_____

_____

_____

_____

_____

_____

_____

_____

_____

Day 10 _____

_____

_____

_____

_____

_____

_____

_____

_____

_____

Day 11

_____

_____

_____

_____

_____

_____

_____

_____

_____

Day 12

_____

_____

_____

_____

_____

_____

_____

_____

_____

_____

Day 13 _____

_____

_____

_____

_____

_____

_____

_____

_____

_____

_____

Day 14 _____

_____

_____

_____

_____

_____

_____

_____

_____

_____

_____

_____

Day 15

_____

_____

_____

_____

_____

_____

_____

_____

_____

Day 16

_____

_____

_____

_____

_____

_____

_____

_____

_____

_____

Day 17

_____
_____
_____
_____
_____
_____
_____
_____
_____
_____

Day 18

_____
_____
_____
_____
_____
_____
_____
_____
_____
_____
_____
_____
_____

Day 19

_____

Day 20

_____

Day 21

_____
_____
_____
_____
_____
_____
_____
_____
_____

Day 22

_____
_____
_____
_____
_____
_____
_____
_____
_____
_____

Day 23 _____

_____

_____

_____

_____

_____

_____

_____

_____

_____

Day 24 _____

_____

_____

_____

_____

_____

_____

_____

_____

_____

_____

Day 25

Day 26

Day 27 _____

_____

_____

_____

_____

_____

_____

_____

_____

_____

Day 28 _____

_____

_____

_____

_____

_____

_____

_____

_____

_____

_____

Day 29

_____

Day 30

_____

MEDITATION #11: COMPASSION

"Our task must be to free ourselves...
by widening our circle of compassion
to embrace all living creatures and the
whole of nature and it's beauty."

~ Albert Einstein~

Compassion

MEDITATION #11: COMPASSION

Embody compassion through this simple meditation.
In every breath feel compassion to yourself and others.

5 short and simple steps:

1. Sit in a comfortable position in a quiet room. Place your hands together to center your mind and set an intention for your practice.

2. Place your hands on your lap. Feel your breath, and with the next inhale lengthen your spine, and when you exhale relax your shoulders. Stay in this position throughout your practice whilst easy breathing.

3. Breathe into your Hara and say, "I breathe in compassion". Breathe out to your Hara and say, "I breathe out compassion". Every breath in and out is with pure intent of compassion to yourself and others.

4. Continue for a few minutes and add extra minutes, as you feel guided.

5. End the practice with gratitude, with hands together saying "thank you".

Incorporate this meditation into your daily activities

- Upon waking up rest in your bed for two minutes. Place your hand in your heart and take a nice slow and deep breath in and say, " I breathe in compassion". As you breath out say, "I breathe out compassion." Continue for three to six rounds.

- During mini breaks sit and relax. Take a moment and bring awareness to your breath. As you breathe in silently say, "I breathe in compassion". As you breath out say, "I breathe out compassion". Continue for three to six rounds.

- Before you go to sleep lie down on your bed. Place your hand in your heart and as you breathe in say," I breathe in compassion". As you breath out say, "I breathe out compassion". Continue for three to six rounds.

On the following pages journal your daily experience practicing the Compassion meditation for the next 30 days

Day 1 _____

_____

_____

_____

_____

_____

_____

_____

_____

_____

_____

Day 2 _____

_____

_____

_____

_____

_____

_____

_____

_____

_____

_____

_____

_____

Day 3 _____

_____

_____

_____

_____

_____

_____

_____

_____

Day 4 _____

_____

_____

_____

_____

_____

_____

_____

_____

Day 5

_____

_____

_____

_____

_____

_____

_____

_____

_____

_____

_____

Day 6

_____

_____

_____

_____

_____

_____

_____

_____

_____

_____

_____

Day 7

_____

Day 8

_____

Day 9 _____

_____

_____

_____

_____

_____

_____

_____

Day 10 _____

_____

_____

_____

_____

_____

_____

_____

_____

Day 11

_____

_____

_____

_____

_____

_____

_____

_____

_____

_____

_____

Day 12

_____

_____

_____

_____

_____

_____

_____

_____

_____

_____

_____

_____

Day 13

_____

_____

_____

_____

_____

_____

_____

_____

_____

_____

_____

Day 14

_____

_____

_____

_____

_____

_____

_____

_____

_____

_____

_____

_____

Day 15 _____

_____

_____

_____

_____

_____

_____

_____

Day 16 _____

_____

_____

_____

_____

_____

_____

_____

Day 17

_____

_____

_____

_____

_____

_____

_____

_____

_____

Day 18

_____

_____

_____

_____

_____

_____

_____

_____

_____

Day 19 _____

_____

_____

_____

_____

_____

_____

_____

_____

Day 20 _____

_____

_____

_____

_____

_____

_____

_____

_____

Day 21 _____

_____

_____

_____

_____

_____

_____

_____

_____

_____

_____

Day 22 _____

_____

_____

_____

_____

_____

_____

_____

_____

_____

_____

Day 23

Day 24

Day 25

_____
_____
_____
_____
_____
_____
_____
_____
_____
_____

Day 26

_____
_____
_____
_____
_____
_____
_____
_____
_____
_____
_____

Day 27

_____

_____

_____

_____

_____

_____

_____

_____

_____

_____

Day 28

_____

_____

_____

_____

_____

_____

_____

_____

_____

_____

Day 29 _____

_____

_____

_____

_____

_____

_____

_____

_____

_____

_____

Day 30 _____

_____

_____

_____

_____

_____

_____

_____

_____

_____

_____

_____

MEDITATION #12: WALKING

"When you walk, arrive with every step.
That is walking meditation.
There's nothing else to it."

~ Thich Nhat Hanh~

Walking

Walking meditation involves a simple walk with breath awareness and being in the present moment.

5 short and simple steps:

1. Stand in a comfortable position in a quiet room with enough space to walk around, or go outdoors into nature. Place your hands together to center your mind and set an intention for your practice.

2. Bring your hands to your side. Inhale and lengthen your spine, and then exhale and relax your shoulders. Maintain this position whilst walking and breathing easily.

3. As you breathe in step one foot, and as you breathe out step the other foot. Every step you make is accompanied with a conscious breath. Feel the ground and earth beneath you. Feel one with the earth.

4. Continue for a few minutes and add extra minutes, as you feel guided.

5. End the practice with gratitude, with hands together saying "thank you".

Incorporate this meditation into your daily activities

- Upon waking up when you get out of bed, bring awareness to your breath. As you step one foot breathe in, then step the other foot and breathe out. Feel your connection to the earth and be grateful. Do this for a few steps and feel grounded.

- During mini breaks have a short walk around the office or in a nice weather go outside. Take a moment and bring awareness to your breath, as you step one foot breathe in, and step the other foot breathe out. Do this for few steps and feel grounded.

- Before you go to sleep walk few steps beside your bed. Bring awareness to your breath. As you place one foot - breathe in, and place the other foot - breath out. Feel your connection to the earth and be grateful. Do this for few steps to feel grounded and relaxed before you sleep

On the following pages journal your daily experience practicing the Walking meditation for the next 30 days

Day 1

_____

_____

_____

_____

_____

_____

_____

_____

_____

_____

_____

_____

_____

Day 2

_____

_____

_____

_____

_____

_____

_____

_____

_____

_____

_____

_____

_____

Day 3

_____

_____

_____

_____

_____

_____

_____

_____

_____

_____

Day 4

_____

_____

_____

_____

_____

_____

_____

_____

_____

_____

_____

Day 5

Day 6

Day 7 _____

_____

_____

_____

_____

_____

_____

_____

_____

_____

Day 8 _____

_____

_____

_____

_____

_____

_____

_____

_____

_____

_____

_____

Day 9

_____

_____

_____

_____

_____

_____

_____

_____

_____

Day 10

_____

_____

_____

_____

_____

_____

_____

_____

_____

_____

_____

Day 11

_____

_____

_____

_____

_____

_____

_____

_____

_____

Day 12

_____

_____

_____

_____

_____

_____

_____

_____

_____

Day 13 _____

_____

_____

_____

_____

_____

_____

_____

_____

_____

_____

Day 14 _____

_____

_____

_____

_____

_____

_____

_____

_____

_____

_____

_____

_____

Day 15

Day 16

Day 17

_____

Day 18

_____

Day 19

Day 20

Day 21

Day 22

Day 23

Day 24

Day 25

_____
_____
_____
_____
_____
_____
_____
_____
_____
_____

Day 26

_____
_____
_____
_____
_____
_____
_____
_____
_____
_____
_____
_____

Day 27

Day 28

Day 29

Day 30

ADDITIONAL PRACTICE
- MORNING GRATITUDE

"The whole process of mental adjustment and atonement can be summed up in one word, gratitude."

"First, you believe that there is one Intelligent Substance, from which all things proceed; second, you believe that this Substance gives you everything you desire; and third, you relate yourself to it by a feeling of deep and profound gratitude."

~ Wallace D. Wattles ~

In addition to these twelve simple and concise meditations, I would like to share with you my daily morning gratitude practice. This regular practice has become one of my essential needs. If for some reason I am unable to practice my morning ritual; I feel my day is not complete and I will not sleep well. Every day this practice is my guide to live my life with purpose, vision and goals. I truly believe this practice of gratitude steers us closer to our source. I am so happy and grateful that I learned this practice through the Bob Proctor Coaching Program.

I call this practice "Morning Gratitude" because I love to start my day with gratitude and affirmations. You can practice gratitude anytime of the day; the morning is ideal for listing all those things you are grateful for; everything you have receive already as well as the things you desire or hope to happen in the future.

Here's a simple guide to Morning Gratitude.

1. Write down ten things that you are grateful for.

List on paper or in your journal notebook ten things that you are grateful for; the things that you already have, and your future wishes. Start by writing, "I am so happy and grateful now that…" Write it in the present tense and feel the gratitude.

2. Ask for guidance to your source (God) or spirit.

After writing your ten gratitudes take five minutes to sit in a comfortable, quiet and peaceful space. Close your eyes and breathe in and out to your Hara for two to three rounds of breath. Feel the connection to your source. When fully engaged start by saying thank you for the blessings you have received and the guidance you have requested. Maintain this composure for a few moments and visualize a bright light above your head, and receive the blessings and guidance from your spirit or source.

Example: "Thank you for all the blessings and abundance you provided for me, my source (spirit or Supreme God). My pure intent today is to live my purpose, vision and goal; to share love, peace and joy to everyone. Provide me with your loving guidance today. I am so grateful for your guidance."

3. Send love to those who concern and perplex you, and cause you anxiety and stress.

Love is very compassionate and understanding. Feel love for yourself first and then feel the love you are receiving. An example of this is the love you receive from your parents, spouse or partner, children and pets. Embody that sensation, and feel that your whole being is radiating with glowing light coming from that pure love. Sometimes this moment of abundant joy in your glowing light of love can falter, when your thoughts turn to an unpleasant experience of a person who bothers or stress you. Trust in the power of that pure love, and eventually your feelings for that person will also turn into gratitude.

I always use the pure and unconditional love that I feel when I am with my dog "Wade". I visualize those moments with Wade; really feel those beautiful happy feelings, and at same time think of the person who bothers and stresses me. I feel a deep interconnectedness as I merge these contrary feelings together, and I send love to the person who bothers me, and I feel peace and joy.

On the following pages take the opportunity
to list everything that you are grateful for

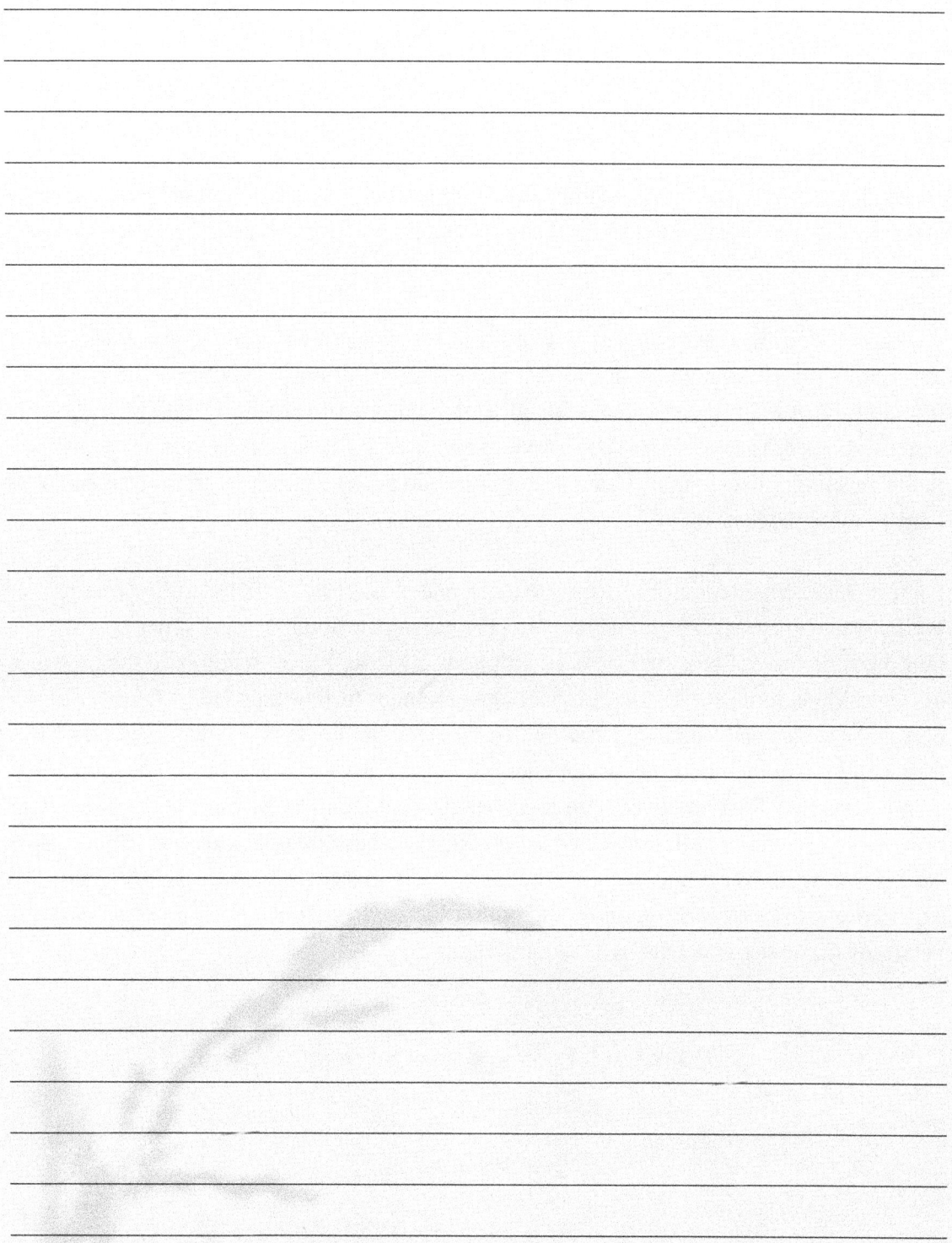

AUTHOR'S BIOGRAPHY

Every day when I wake up in the morning I will start with the affirmation "I am so happy and grateful now for another beautiful day to live my purpose and achieve my goals. I will share love, joy and peace to everyone I connect with today."

It's a lovely feeling to start the day with a smile and a positive attitude. During that time, I am reciting my affirmations in my mind. I also visualize my purpose, visions, goals and the love, joy and peace I share to others. My affirmation is also my intention, and with my daily visualizations I also add a short and sweet meditation. I also have a passion for journaling in the morning; I list ten things I am grateful for, the ones I have already received and ones I am about to receive.

I am a Yoga, Meditation, and Reiki teacher and a Success Accountability partner for Wellness and Personal Development. I am very passionate about helping super busy people find the time for wellness, personal growth and self-care. I love to combine the practices of Yoga, Meditation, Reiki and Personal Development to find balance in my life. In my personal practice and teaching, I start with a short meditation to calm my mind and body. I truly believe that in order to focus our energy we must first focus our mind. The foundation of my Yoga and Reiki practices are meditation. Meditation is an amazing practice that brings us to a state of stillness. When we are still, we become one with everything; when we are one with everything, we feel the deep interconnectedness with the universe. We experience calmness, peace and joy, and our minds are free from distractions and worries. I start my day and end my day with a calm mind.

Thank you for sharing your practice with me.

www.ingramcontent.com/pod-product-compliance
Lightning Source LLC
Chambersburg PA
CBHW081227090426
42738CB00016B/3217